Answering the Call of Faith

DERRICK G. BLUE

Copyright © 2015 Derrick Blue

All rights reserved.

ISBN: 978-0-9971073-0-2

ACKNOWLEDGMENTS

First, I thank God for His Son Jesus. He is the reason that I am who I am. I can't even begin to fully express who He is to me.

Next, I feel extremely privileged and grateful for my parents. It is the spiritual guidance I received from them that truly has directed my path. I am also thankful for the teaching I have received from my Church of God by Faith, Inc. family. It has trained and continues to equip me for this work I am called to do.

I realize that when God gives you an assignment he provides you with the means of accomplishing it. I see clearly that he has consistently placed people in my life who have demonstrated His love and favor toward me. I am grateful.

Special Thanks:

Rena Fish- Editor
Sherilyn Michelle Bennett- Cover Design

DEDICATION

This book is dedicated to my wife, Melanie Lynette Blue. I could think of no other person who personifies love and care like my Mel. I am what I am becoming because of her. Nothing on this earth makes me feel more complete than knowing she is with me. Every struggle and obstacle has shown us what Love is, for Love is God. I salute a loving wife and awesome mother. This is for you, Mel!

Thank you for everything.

D

CONTENTS

1	Total Submission	Pg 4
2	The Essence of Expectation	Pg 9
3	Spiritual Economics	Pg 17
4	The Law of Faith	Pg 20
5	Step out of the Comfort Zone	Pg 28
6	A Saved Man: Where God Lives	Pg 36
7	What if He doesn't do it?	Pg 42
8	Is that your final answer?	Pg 46

Introduction

I know what you're thinking–another book about God. Another book telling me how to have my desires fulfilled in seven easy steps. Another book about how I can get rich by simply praying a prayer. Well, I am so sorry to disappoint you. This book is an alarm. The book is a challenge to everyone who would take the time to read it. This book is here to engage your thinking at a different level and cause you to reconsider everything you have been taught. This book is a mirror in which you can see yourself.

Maybe you are a skeptic who's not into the "God stuff," and you have questions and doubts concerning Christianity. Perhaps the scrutiny in the media and the scandals among religious leaders is causing you to doubt the validity of Christianity. As a result, you've grouped all religious leaders into one category…..fake.

Maybe you're a believer who knows that there must be more to life. Maybe you're one who has questions. Why did mom die? Why did I lose my job? Why was my sister raped? Why haven't we been able to have children? Why does God allow such great tragedy to take place? While this book may not answer these questions, it will certainly point you to the answer–Christ.

Faith is more than having a thorough knowledge of the Bible or the ability to tickle the ears of the church with a catch phrase and an organ. This call is evidenced through a faithful life. This call is an inner conviction that drives the believer. For without faith, we are in a hopeless state. To live a life believing only in the things that are seen is discouraging to a person who has many questions.

God has placed a desire to know Him inside each of us. Many search for Him through scientific ideology or religions. But the truth of the matter is, access to God is only granted through faith in Jesus Christ.

It's important to understand that the desire to find out more is completely normal. God placed the desire–or the void– inside you to push you to search. It's the still, small voice calling you to a place beyond yourself and into intimacy with your Creator. It's the call of faith.

"And without faith it is impossible to please God, because anyone who comes to him must believe that he exists and that he rewards those who earnestly seek him" (Hebrews 11:6 NIV).

So our goal should be to live by faith. As elementary as this may sound, faith is often the missing element in the lives of professing Christians. Christians must do more than believe that there is a God. We should live like there is a God.

Imagine how crazy it would be to see a police officer who lawfully wears the badge, carries the gun, and possesses the authority to work as an officer but does not exercise the authority. God is telling us that He has given us the authority.

ANSWERING THE CALL OF FAITH

DERRICK G. BLUE

TOTAL SUBMISSION

"I beseech you therefore, brethren, by the mercies of God, that ye present your bodies a living sacrifice, holy, acceptable unto God, which is your reasonable service."

Romans 12:1

LET GO AND LET GOD!

ANSWERING THE CALL OF FAITH

In 1999 I accepted Christ as my personal Savior. During the days surrounding my salvation, I found myself asking questions about faith. I found myself praying for faith and asking God, "What is faith?" I knew the Bible said to have faith, but how? I knew that my life was new and different, but what about faith? How could I have something that I didn't understand? In order to answer the call of faith, one must first attempt to understand what faith is. What is the role and purpose of faith in my life?

Faith is more than a religion or just something that helps us get the blessings of God. The primary purpose of faith is the salvation of our souls. Faith in the work of the cross is the vehicle that carries us from death to life. It's more than just lip service. Faith is realizing our inability, then trusting in God's ability. Faith is realizing we can't survive without God.

True faith is total submission to God through Christ. I cannot truly believe in something to which I am not submitted. My faith calls me to action.

A good definition of *submission* is "to empty out our own agenda and become subject to another's agenda." The word *sub* speaks to "being under," and *mission* defined is "a focused course of action." So essentially, *submission* means "being under a mission." Total submission is completely embracing God's way of living. It's being under the influence and control of God.

You can put water inside of a glass, but that does not make it full. When the glass is full, nothing else can be poured into it. You can be saved and have the Holy Spirit but not work to the full potential intended by God.

God is asking, even desiring our full attention. Baptism is a symbol of submission.

Baptism is an outward expression of a spiritual change. As believers, we are granted access to operate in a spiritual realm through faith. When I am taken under (meaning accept Christ as my personal Savior), my old nature is buried; and when I am pulled out, I am washed of the world's impurities, limits, and restrictions. Symbolically, the old me dies in the water. I have now gained a freedom to operate in the power and authority of God in the newness of life.

Baptism is a picture of a death. Death means, I no longer live according to the pattern of the world and I no longer embrace ideas and concepts that are contrary to God's Word.

It's shocking to hear many of the messages from the pulpit. There is such a strong emphasis on getting rich and on the idea that the lack of wealth equates to lack of faith. I am not opposed to financial teaching, and I understand that giving precedes receiving, but God would rather you be poor by the world's standards than to be spiritually bankrupt.

As we submit to God, we connect to His authority, His provision, and His strength. We are an extension of what we are submitted to. Submission to God brings power to the believer.

"Submit yourselves, then, to God. Resist the devil, and he will flee from you" (James 4:7 NIV).

Submission gives you the power to resist sin. Defeat comes when you have not submitted to God. By submission, we come under the authority of God.

OFF THE PAGES AND INTO YOUR LIFE: A TIME OF PERSONAL REFLECTION

Think about areas in your life that you know you have not submitted to God. List them below or write them on a separate sheet of paper. *For Example, an inappropriate relationship, a bad habit or un-forgiveness etc.*

Now that you have written them down, answer these questions:

1. Are these things worth my peace of mind or peace with God?

2. If they were not in my life where would I be? How would I be living?

The Prayer of Faith

Father, I realize that I am powerless without you. I cannot succeed without your power and might. I thank you for giving me access to freedom. Today I choose freedom and I denounce the things that have kept me defeated. I submit today, not just in words, but in action. I pray that the Holy Spirit would prevail in my heart. Please remind me daily that I am a champion through Christ and that I have victory. Today I bow in total submission. In Jesus' name, Amen

THE ESSENCE OF EXPECTATION

"Now unto him that is able to do exceeding abundantly above all that we ask or think, according to the power that worketh in us"

Ephesians 3:20

HOW BIG IS GOD...IN YOU?

In building a house, the foundation determines how large the house will be. A house will only be as large as the foundation.

Often people look at faith as a blind leap into the unknown, but I beg to differ. We walk by faith, and not by sight. We are led by an invisible conviction that cannot be seen. Although we cannot see, we rest assured that God sees. When I think about the essence of expectation, I think of an empty glass; this symbolizes our hope and expectation. What does an empty glass do besides take up space? A glass was made for a purpose; this purpose is to be filled with a substance, and the glass will not profit anyone while empty. As Proverbs explains, "Hope deferred maketh the heart sick: but *when* the desire cometh, *it is* a tree of life" (Proverbs 13:12).

There is nothing more frustrating than wishing and hoping for something and then realizing that you can't have it.

Hebrews 11:1 sheds light on this principle: "Now faith is the substance of things hoped for, the evidence of things not seen."

So we understand that faith is a substance. It is what fills our empty hopes. It is the essence of our expectation.

ANSWERING THE CALL OF FAITH

Mark 5: 24-34

[24] And Jesus went with him; and much people followed him, and thronged him.

[25] And a certain woman, which had an issue of blood twelve years,

[26] And had suffered many things of many physicians, and had spent all that she had, and was nothing bettered, but rather grew worse,

[27] When she had heard of Jesus, came in the press behind, and touched his garment.

[28] For she said, If I may touch but his clothes, I shall be whole.

[29] And straightway the fountain of her blood was dried up; and she felt in her body that she was healed of that plague.

[30] And Jesus, immediately knowing in himself that virtue had gone out of him, turned him about in the press, and said, Who touched my clothes?

[31] And his disciples said unto him, Thou seest the multitude thronging thee, and sayest thou, Who touched me?

[32] And he looked round about to see her that had done this thing.

[33] But the woman fearing and trembling, knowing what was done in her, came and fell down before him, and told him all the truth.

[34] And he said unto her, Daughter, thy faith hath made thee whole; go in peace, and be whole of thy plague.

As we study this passage, we see a woman who had an issue of blood. Her very life was departing from her body for twelve long, agonizing years. Doctors could not help her, friends walked out; all of her money was spent, and she had exhausted all of her resources.

If we, for a moment, put the spotlight on her, we can extract some very important principles in our challenge to answer the call of faith.

The woman in the story had many challenges. First, she was a woman in a man's world! Second, she was considered unclean because of her condition. Even in the midst of what appeared to be disadvantages, her faith prevailed.

Notice the following principles:

1. She **heard** – She got to the place where Jesus would be. Position yourself to connect with God. (Mark 5:27)

2. She **said** – The woman had to encourage herself. "For she said, If I may touch but his clothes, I shall be whole." (Mark 5:28) Learn to speak the results you need.

3. She **pressed** – The woman displayed a spiritual toughness. She pressed her way through crowds of people. She dealt with criticism and overcame pride (Mark 5:27).

In order to receive from God, we must not let the opinions of people hinder us. We must adopt the by-any-means-necessary mentality.

4. She **received** – Immediately she received her healing. (Mark 5:29)

By applying these principles on a daily basis, we can see positive results. She didn't wait for Jesus to touch her; she touched him.

OFF THE PAGES AND INTO YOUR LIFE: A TIME OF PERSONAL REFLECTION

Expectation

ekspek'tāSH(ə)n/

noun

1.   a strong belief that something will happen or be the case in the future

Source: www.merriam-webster.com/dictionary

Two things often govern our expectations:

1. History (Things we have experienced whether positive or negative)
2. God's word

What negative things in your past keep you from believing God for a better today? List them below or write them on a separate sheet of paper? *For Example, you may have been in a relationship that ended badly. Maybe you were abused, rejected or disappointed by family or people you trusted.*

Read these scriptures:

Jeremiah 29:11 - For I know the thoughts that I think toward you, saith the LORD, thoughts of peace, and not of evil, to give you an expected end.

Proverbs 23:18 - For surely there is an end; and thine expectation shall not be cut off.

Psalms 62:5 - My soul, wait thou only upon God; for my expectation [is] from him.

Philippians 1:20 - According to my earnest expectation and [my] hope, that in nothing I shall be ashamed, but [that] with all boldness, as always, [so] now also Christ shall be magnified in my body, whether [it be] by life, or by death.

The Prayer of Faith

Father, I have let my history effect my present and it has caused me not to believe your word as I should. Today I ask that you forgive me. I have put you on the same level as man. You are not the author of my pain, you are the healer of my soul. Help me to forget the past disappointments and embrace your plans for me. I declare that I am not a victim of my past. I expect all that your Word says is mine. I am not a beggar, I am a child of God. In Jesus' name. Amen.

DERRICK G. BLUE

SPIRITUAL ECONOMICS

"For he that cometh to God must believe that he is, and that he is a rewarder of them that diligently seek him."

Hebrews 11:6b

THE SPIRITUAL LAW OF SUPPLY AND DEMAND

In economics, there is a foundational principle that is called the law of supply and demand. This law says that demand (the desire to possess a commodity or make use of a service combined with the ability to obtain it) creates supply (the amount of a commodity available).

The laws of the Kingdom of God are very similar. There must be a demand for the things of God. The Bible says, "Blessed are they which do hunger and thirst after righteousness: for they shall be filled" (Matthew 5:6).

The hunger creates the filling. God has an unlimited supply of virtue to release to us, but we must put a demand on that power. People who experience deliverance in their lives are people who understand this fact.

My father, Emanuel Roberts Sr., preached a message many years ago that sticks with me even today. His topic was, "You Get What You Pay For." He was saying that you must have a persistent spiritual life to experience true victory. You cannot neglect prayer and a regular devotion to God and expect spiritual results. The words of the Bible are compared to seeds; the seeds must be first planted and then constantly watered and cultivated. This is true of our spiritual life.

The economy of the Kingdom of God is faith. Faith produces healing; faith produces breakthroughs and deliverance from the things that trouble us. But remember, faith comes to us when we have a true desire to hear the Word of God. Faith needs to be grown; it won't just grow.

OFF THE PAGES AND INTO YOUR LIFE: A TIME OF PERSONAL REFLECTION

An essential part of living by faith is seeking God. It means we must seek Him, not just what He can do.

Seek His heart, not just His hand.

Today I challenge you to change the tone of your prayers. Set aside time every day to ask God for a closer walk with Him. Avoid praying for money and other monetary things. Instead pray for things like:

- Right living.
- Right thinking.
- Spiritual purity and holiness.
- Accompany this with designated time to study the Word of God.

The Prayer of Faith

Father, your word says, "Blessed are they which do hunger and thirst after righteous". I ask today that you would help me to have a sincere hunger for you and the things that please you. According to your word, you know what I need before I ask, so today I am seeking your kingdom and your righteousness. Fill me with your righteousness. Search my heart, and take out those things that are not like you. In Jesus name. Amen.

DERRICK G. BLUE

THE LAW OF FAITH

"Now faith is the substance of things hoped for, the evidence of things not seen."

Hebrews 11:1

FAITH'S JUDICIAL SYSTEM

Two laws are at work in our lives: the laws of nature and the law of faith. In any government or system, there is law. When I say *government*, I mean "an established way of living." The word *law* means "the rule of action, considered to be binding by the authoritative administration."

To bring clarity to what I'm saying, I will use the following illustration. Let's compare road rules to aviation rules. In an automobile, I am obligated to obey the laws of the highway, such as stop signs, speed limits, traffic lights, and so on. All these laws are right and used to keep people safe when operating a motor vehicle on the highway. But if I were to fly a plane, I do not have to abide by these same rules. A stop sign would do me no good in a plane. Even though road rules do not apply to me while I'm flying a plane, road rules are still in effect, but only in another realm. I cannot mix these two laws. They are two different laws, yet one doesn't cancel the other.

I know that a car can only take me to the airport, just as the natural laws can only take me so far. When it comes to healing, faith doesn't say sickness is not there. How would I know I'm sick if the symptoms were not there? What faith says is that even though sickness is there, faith is there also, and faith says I'm healed. My faith is stronger than my sickness. My conviction is stronger than my condition. It is important to understand that despite the circumstances, God is the final authority and supreme decision maker.

His intervention in natural affairs makes the difference. This is the law of faith. If we can attach our mind and heart to this principle, we will never be defeated.

The "IT" Factor

What if I told you that you were on trial? The verdict had already been decided in your favor, but you still had to go on with the proceedings. How would you react during the trial? How would you act knowing you had already won the case? In the justice system, any conviction requires evidence, or it's unjust. Two thousand years ago the mission of Christ was accomplished. Jesus said, "It is finished" and gave us the victory.

"When Jesus therefore had received the vinegar, he said, It is finished: and he bowed his head, and gave up the ghost" (John19:30).

What did the "IT" mean for us? The "IT" meant his work was complete.

In any courtroom, a verdict is found based on:

1. **Evidence** – an outward sign, something that furnishes proof: something legally submitted to ascertain the truth of a matter. As Christians, we have two forms of evidence that form our conviction.

The first is the evidence of the cross, Jesus' death and resurrection. This evidence is undisputable and immutable.

In some churches I've seen and visited, I was made to feel ashamed because I didn't dance, yell, shout, or act a certain way. These actions were supposedly the evidence of my salvation. The true evidence of your faith is your lifestyle. Your lifestyle is your total being. This is how you believe, think, act, and operate. To sum it all up, you live like you believe. Your faith is displayed and validated through your life.

2. **Witness** - attestation of a fact or event. Any credible witness must have experienced or seen something that gives him his conclusion. Are you a true witness? Have you allowed God to come into your life?

In the courtroom, a witness can make or break the case. People can see if a person has truly experienced a thing. It is a certain confidence that is conveyed through the words he says. A true witness has been affected emotionally, psychologically, and most of all spiritually by the thing of which he speaks.

3. **Testimony** - a solemn declaration, usually made orally by a witness under oath in response to interrogation. A testimony is an open acknowledgment or public profession. The testimony of a person is usually important in every court case. The verdict of a court case can be adversely affected by testimony.

In dealing with faith, testimony is of the utmost importance. The Bible is an entire book of testimonies.

Faith comes by hearing. Hearing what? It's hearing the testimony of God about Himself and the testimony of others about God. "So then faith cometh by hearing, and hearing by the word of God" (Romans 10:17).

A witness speaks and makes a verbal confession. The Bible declares: "That if thou shalt confess with thy mouth the Lord Jesus, and shalt believe in thine heart that God hath raised him from the dead, thou shalt be saved" (Romans 10:9). Contextually, this speaks of saving faith, but remember, there is one faith! The faith that saves is the faith that heals and delivers.

Faith is about what you say based on what you've seen and heard. Testimony can only be received from a witness. If you haven't accepted Jesus, you are not a witness. The apostles were able to speak with power because they had been with Jesus; they experienced God.

So when we deal with trials and various struggles, we know that the case has already gone before God, our judge, and Jesus our lawyer has won the case. With that being said, God wants us to live like winners.

OFF THE PAGES AND INTO YOUR LIFE: A TIME OF PERSONAL REFLECTION

Sometimes bad news can impact our belief system. Our human nature responds by what is heard and we determine whether to embrace it or reject it. Have you ever received a doctor's report that was really negative? Every symptom to the report was visible and the proof was evident. What do you do?

Write down things in your life that are not where you want it to be. List them below or write them on a separate sheet of paper. This time I want you to make a chart. (See below) *For Example, list things like: my spouse or loved one is unsaved. I can't find a job. My finances are a wreck. My marriage is in trouble. I have been diagnosed with cancer or some other sickness.*

My Situation	God's Promise	My Confession
I have been out of work for a while. My bills are stacking up and I really don't know what to do.	Humble yourselves, therefore, under God's mighty hand, that he may lift you up in due time. Cast all your anxiety on him because he cares for you. I Peter 5:6-7	Lord, thank you for understanding my need. I realize that you will make a way for me in due time. I am your child and you will provide for me.
My child(ren) or spouse are unsaved and it makes it hard for me.	For the Son of man is come to seek and to save that which was lost. Luke 19:10	Lord, thank you, you are seeking to save my family.
My bills are more than my income and often it is difficult to make ends meet.	[26] Behold the fowls of the air: for they sow not, neither do they reap, nor gather into barns; yet your heavenly Father feedeth them. Are ye not much better than they? Matthew 6:26	Lord, thank you, I do not have to worry. If you provide for the fowls, I know you will provide for me.
I am sick	But He was wounded for our transgressions, He was bruised for our iniquities; The chastisement for our peace was upon Him, And *by His stripes* we are healed. Isaiah 53:5	Lord, thank you. I acknowledge that your stripes have healed me. I now wait in expectation for the manifestation in my body.

The Prayer of Faith

Father, you know my heart. You know my struggles. I have decided that I will not dwell on my problem, I will confess your promise. Your word declares that you speak those things that are not as though they were. I choose to believe your report. It is my faith that makes me whole. So I confess that everything that is contrary and promotes fear in my life must line up and comply to your word. In Jesus' name. Amen.

STEP OUT OF THE COMFORT ZONE

"Who against hope believed in hope, that he might become the father of many nations; according to that which was spoken, So shall thy seed be."

Romans 4:18

Operating in faith sometimes requires us to leave the familiar and comfortable and venture into another realm. The children of Israel were given divine instructions from God to possess the Promised Land. However, the land was occupied by other nations. They were given the land, but they had to possess it.

Read the text below, found in Numbers chapter 13, to paint the picture:

[1] And the LORD spake unto Moses, saying,

[2] Send thou men, that they may search the land of Canaan, which I give unto the children of Israel: of every tribe of their fathers shall ye send a man, every one a ruler among them.

[18] And see the land, what it is, and the people that dwelleth therein, whether they be strong or weak, few or many;

[19] And what the land is that they dwell in, whether it be good or bad; and what cities they be that they dwell in, whether in tents, or in strong holds;

[20] And what the land is, whether it be fat or lean, whether there be wood therein, or not. And be ye of good courage, and bring of the fruit of the land. Now the time was the time of the first ripe grapes.

[21] So they went up, and searched the land from the wilderness of Zin unto Rehob, as men come to Hamath.

²⁵ And they returned from searching of the land after forty days.

²⁶ And they went and came to Moses, and to Aaron, and to all the congregation of the children of Israel, unto the wilderness of Paran, to Kadesh; and brought back word unto them, and unto all the congregation, and shewed them the fruit of the land.

²⁷ And they told him, and said, We came unto the land whither thou sentest us, and surely it floweth with milk and honey; and this is the fruit of it.

²⁸ Nevertheless the people be strong that dwell in the land, and the cities are walled, and very great: and moreover we saw the children of Anak there.

²⁹ The Amalekites dwell in the land of the south: and the Hittites, and the Jebusites, and the Amorites, dwell in the mountains: and the Canaanites dwell by the sea, and by the coast of Jordan.

³⁰ And Caleb stilled the people before Moses, and said, Let us go up at once, and possess it; for we are well able to overcome it.

³¹ But the men that went up with him said, We be not able to go up against the people; for they are stronger than we.

When you read those verses, you should see something that is abundantly clear. Faith isn't everything falling into your lap. Having faith is first believing and then maintaining the same conviction despite contradicting circumstances.

I hope you understand that there is first a promise from God. Next, there are instructions regarding the corresponding actions. After, there is a choice. The children of Israel were left with an option to bow out gracefully or to possess that which had already been given to them.

What do you do when you are confronted with challenges that don't seem to line up with what you think God is telling you to do? Do you pursue, even with the challenges? Do you conclude that what you were praying for must not have been God's will because things didn't work as planned?

Every great man and woman of faith has a vast resume of trials to his/her credit as well. You will recognize God's power in you when your strength runs out. I'm not saying that God doesn't want us to be comfortable in life. What I'm saying is, if we never move out of our comfort zone, we may miss what God has for us.

The Next Level

Since I can remember, I have heard the phrase, "Let's go to the next level." The truth of the matter is, God is always trying to take us higher. He's always calling us to higher levels of commitment and faith, but it's more than just a catch phrase.

The next level means going to a different level, a new level. As you press toward greater things, you leave old things and embrace new things. Fear is an enemy of faith. However, they are alike in that they are both responses to hearing. Caleb and Joshua heard and saw the same things as the other spies, but they responded differently than the others. Their fear overshadowed their ability to believe. God wants to take us to a new level, but sometimes the discomfort we experience is not because we missed God's will; it's because we are at a new level.

Let's examine Peter's walking on water. Matthew 14:29-32 contains this story.

[29] And he said, Come. And when Peter was come down out of the ship, he walked on the water, to go to Jesus.

[30] But when he saw the wind boisterous, he was afraid; and beginning to sink, he cried, saying, Lord, save me.

[31] And immediately Jesus stretched forth his hand, and caught him, and said unto him, O thou of little faith, wherefore didst thou doubt?

[32] And when they were come into the ship, the wind ceased.

Peter went from the natural realm to the spiritual realm through faith. He was first supported by the boat, and then Jesus called him to another level beyond the boat through

His Word. He was no longer supported by the tangible, but by God's word.

Going to the next level means:

1. Understanding where I am now. Have I mastered and maximized my current place?

2. Being prepared to be persecuted and misunderstood.

3. Staying focused in spite of your circumstances.

4. Not being afraid to fail. Failure doesn't always mean "never"; it could mean "not now" or "not ready."

5. Using the fear, awkwardness, or discomfort you feel as fuel to propel you forward into the arms of Christ.

Support System

Crutches are necessary for injured people who can't use their legs properly without some type of support due to injury. Training wheels, on the other hand, are used to support the undeveloped limbs of a child who will eventually learn to ride a bike on his own.

With this in mind, we have two types of people: injured and undeveloped. Injured people are afraid to do anything out of the norm because comfortable is easy and safe. Comfortable means, "I won't look like a complete idiot if I fail, so why try?"

Maybe you went full steam into a business idea or relationship and you came out injured financially, emotionally, or spiritually. Now you ride with your foot on the brake and keep it safe. Are you injured?

On the other hand, some people are undeveloped. These people want to experience God in unimaginable ways but do not have the insight. They often become discouraged and could eventually become injured.

These people are on spiritual training wheels. They may experience the frustration of feeling as if everyone else is prosperous and flourishing, while they are barely getting along. Maybe God has allowed you to be in training so that He can teach you how to operate outside of the realm of trial and error and inside the realm of faith.

OFF THE PAGES AND INTO YOUR LIFE: A TIME OF PERSONAL REFLECTION

Do not let momentary discomfort cause you to stop pursuing God's best for you.

Think about some issues that you can't seem to get past no matter how hard you try.

Perhaps things like:

- Uncontrollable anger
- Sexual sin
- Peer Pressure
- An addiction

The Prayer of Faith

Father, you know my heart. There is nothing that can be hidden from you. So I come honestly and in humility. These things have allowed me to begin to sink. I need your help. Forgive me, and cleanse me from all unrighteousness. In Jesus name. Amen.

DERRICK G. BLUE

A SAVED MAN: WHERE GOD LIVES

"Know ye not that ye are the temple of God, and that the Spirit of God dwelleth in you?"

1 Corinthians 3:16

Inside of every human is a place reserved for God. Many people fill that space with other things, but it's important to know that the void God created was designed to allow us to seek Him. This is the plan of free agency and volition.

In the beginning, God created man, and in order to give man life, God breathed Himself into man, because God is life. After man's fall, we needed to be reconnected and then breathed into again; this is the indwelling of the Holy Ghost.

We understand that the Trinity – Father, Son, and the Holy Ghost – are one. God has designed this in a way that He can live in us and through us. If God truly lives in us, then His will is to be in complete control of our lives.

We were designed to be a house for God to live in on Earth.

"Ye are of God, little children, and have overcome them: because greater is he that is in you, than he that is in the world" (I John 4:4).

He lives in us. We do not have Him; He has us. We were bought with a price. If I bought a car, it's mine. I do not belong to the car.

A Matter of the Heart

In the human body, the heart is the central point. The heart circulates blood to every organ in the body. Once the heart stops pumping, the body begins to shut down. Love is the focal point of our faith. Love empowers our faith.

"For in Jesus Christ neither circumcision availeth any thing, nor uncircumcision; but faith which worketh by love" (Galatians 5:6b).

Once love shuts down, peace shuts down, gentleness shuts down, joy shuts down and faith shuts down.

The Bible says God is love. (I John 4:8) Therefore, everything in the life of a believer should be motivated by love. If we do not have love, as the Bible describes, we will live an unfruitful, defeated life.

As we endeavor to see the deep things of God, we must first conquer the surface, the elementary concepts of our walk with Christ. The common theme in the modern church is the idea that God wants to see you blessed (typically monetarily). He does, but if you never get rich, you must understand that He still wants you to receive and reflect His love.

If faith is the car, love is the engine. Our faith will not move us to where we need to be without the love of God motivating it. When we know that love is in us, we know that God is in us. The apostle Paul said that Love is the greatest gift. It is even greater than faith.

"And now abideth faith, hope, charity, these three; but the greatest of these is charity" (I Corinthians 13:13).

Hearing Faith

A commercial from a popular cellular phone company coined a phrase to advertise the reliability of their service in virtually any location. The spokesperson would be in some of the oddest locations and ask the question, "Can you hear me now? Good."

Knowing that God hears us gives us great comfort. Of course I know that God can hear everything, but prayers can be hindered because of disobedience to Him.

I was raised in a home that didn't always have the luxuries of cable or satellite television service; what we had was a television connected by a wire to a tall antenna outside. There would be times that the reception on the screen was fuzzy or blurry. So my grandparents would ask me to go outside and turn the antenna to another position until the reception cleared up.

Many times this is our problem: we are connected but out of position. If we wish to be aligned with God, we have to position ourselves through obedience.

A proper position not only helps us to hear God, but it also allows us to have the power to obey. Everyday distractions can cause our spirit to become so distorted and out of whack. As a result, we don't know who's talking to us – God or the flesh! This is why prayer and studying the word of God are vital to spiritual development.

What Does Faith Look Like?

Let me pose a question. Could someone conclude just by watching you that you were a person of faith? Faith has attributes; faith becomes visible before what we desire becomes visible.

Luke 5:19-20 speaks about a couple of friends who were trying to get another friend, who was lame, to a building where Jesus was. "And when they could not find by what way they might bring him in because of the multitude, they went upon the housetop, and let him down through the tiling with his couch into the midst before Jesus. And when he saw their faith, he said unto him, Man, thy sins are forgiven thee."

After trying all the conventional methods of entrance, they decided to get him there by any means necessary. They climbed on the roof, peeled away the tile, and lowered him down through the roof. The Scripture explains that Jesus "saw" their faith and gave them what they were seeking Him for.

So the first principle here is that faith can be seen. I'm sure many people were wondering what those guys were doing. But we must understand that desperate people do desperate things. Desperation caused Jacob to persevere until he got the blessing he needed. Desperation caused a woman to crawl through crowds of people to touch the hem of her Healer's garment. Faith is seen.

My prayer is that we can learn what our faith should look like and find the answer to the questions that many of us secretly ask God and ourselves: Do I have faith? Am I operating in faith? What should I be doing concerning my request that would show my faith?

Show Me Something

"Yea, a man may say, Thou hast faith, and I have works: shew me thy faith without thy works, and I will shew thee my faith by my works" (Ephesians 2:18).

A small town was experiencing a drought. Consistent 100-degree weather caused concerns to grow and plunged the town into a state of panic. The locals came together to discuss what they were going to do for food. Crops and livestock were dying, and the local economy was suffering. Suddenly, to the surprise of many, an old lady came to the meeting hall wearing a raincoat and boots and holding an umbrella! Surely this woman is crazy, they thought. One of the citizens asked her, "Lady, why are you dressed like that?" But her words changed the whole course of this meeting. She said, "Didn't we pray for rain?"

Are we praying but not expecting? What is the proof of your belief? Faith is more than saying something and it happens; faith is visible; it's a substance, something you can see. Faith is demonstrated. Show me something.

WHAT IF HE DOESN'T DO IT?

"But if not, be it known unto thee, O king, that we will not serve thy gods, nor worship the golden image which thou has set up."

Daniel 3:18

One of the most common questions in the Christian faith is "What if God doesn't do it?" What if, after we have prayed for healing, mom still dies, or the cancer is still there? What if I don't get the job? Did my faith work?

Many will not address this question for fear of losing church members, fame, and money. The fact is, there are things that God will permit to happen because He is God. If we understood as He understood, we wouldn't need Him. His thoughts are not our thoughts. Consider the story of Shadrach, Meshach, and Abednego found in Daniel 3:16-18.

^{16} Shadrach, Meshach, and Abednego, answered and said to the king, O Nebuchadnezzar, we are not careful to answer thee in this matter.

^{17} If it be so, our God whom we serve is able to deliver us from the burning fiery furnace, and he will deliver us out of thine hand, O king.

^{18} But if not, be it known unto thee, O king, that we will not serve thy gods, nor worship the golden image which thou hast set up.

Shadrach, Meshach and Abednego made an astounding statement in the book of Daniel. They refused to compromise their faith for the sake of political or social correctness. As a result, they were thrown into a furnace.

What is true faith? Surely if these men had faith, they would not have been thrown in the furnace. Right?

These three men understood true faith. If God doesn't bring me out, I still believe! Can you say that? Shadrach, Meshach, and Abednego chose to believe God rather than live with the guilt of compromise.

Another man whose life strikes a chord in my mind is Job. The Bible says he was perfect and upright. Surely a perfect and upright man would have a perfect life. The truth of the matter is, this man lost everything dear to him, including his health. Listen to what he says in the midst of a life- changing series of events.

"Though he slay me, yet will I trust in him: but I will maintain mine own ways before him" (Job 13:15).

Job said something that allows us to see what true faith is. With tears in his eyes, he looked to heaven and said, "Though he slay me, yet will I trust him." What was he actually saying? How do his words help us in this faith walk?

Job had accepted the fact that God is sovereign. Although we know that God was not going to slay him, Job didn't. He had so much faith and confidence in God that he was convinced that even if God chose to kill him, he still trusted God and maintained his walk of righteousness. Authentic faith will stand tall in the midst of persecution, sickness, and adversity. Authentic faith will shine through the darkest nights and proclaim that Jesus is Lord. So here's a question for you to think about: What if God doesn't do what you ask?

DERRICK G. BLUE

IS THAT YOUR FINAL ANSWER?

"What shall we then say to these things? If God be for us, who can be against us?"

Romans 8:31

On a famous game show, the contestants are asked a series of questions. Then contestants submit their answer. The host always asks, "Is that your final answer?" Many contestants have lost or won a fortune in this intense moment of the show. This is when you had to know the answer. Everything is on the line. Just like on this game, we experience times when the pressure is on and all our lifelines are used up, and we have to be confident enough to say, "I believe God; that is my final answer."

God has always asked questions to his church. When Adam sinned in the Garden of Eden, God asked Adam, "Where are you?" Later, God asked Ezekiel if the dry bones could live?

Understand that God was asking Ezekiel a question concerning the nation. He didn't ask the king, and he didn't ask the people; he asked his representative, the prophet. God knew that Ezekiel possessed the answer.

There will be a time when your prayer partners will be gone and the people and things that serve as a crutch to you will be unavailable.

I once read the following epigram: Fear knocked on the door; Faith answered, and no one was there. Faith is the air we breathe in the Kingdom of God. When cancer sticks its ugly head up, faith answers, "By His stripes, I'm healed."

When we lack in our finances, faith says that God will supply our every need. Let faith answer life's hard questions. Faith is the force that will stand up in us against the forces of evil when we truly submit ourselves to God. David, when he arose to fight the dreaded champion Goliath, refused to wear Saul's armor. Like David, we should not be weighed down with other people's limitations and insecurities as we fight life's battles.

David's real giant was not the massive nine-foot-tall Philistine that stood before him; no, that was God's battle. But David's giant was deciding to obey God rather than the majority. Goliath was a choice, not a threat. Isn't it true that our biggest challenges and opposition are internal rather than external, within rather than without?

Every challenge in life is a question. Life asks you, Where is your faith? Life asks you, do you really believe in the power and ability of God? The call of faith is all about God's bringing us to a deeper level of commitment and trust in Him.

Today we are confronted with many different heresies, cults, false prophets, men claiming to be Jesus, and all manner of darkness. The enemy is trying to contaminate the spiritual DNA that has been associated with the church.

Satan, in a last-minute, desperate attempt to confuse and deceive, has been conjuring up lies about Jesus, God, and anything that could cause man to know the truth about our Creator and Redeemer. Man has somehow concluded in his small, finite mind that he can understand and decode the so-called hidden truth of God.

I am concerned that we (the twenty-first century church) have not challenged the enemies of our confession.

We have tried to live in harmony with them. We have "had church" instead of being the church. We have allowed political affiliation to override our religious conviction. We have accepted lifestyles that God forbids for the sake of solidifying the socio-economic status in our country.

Many have been strictly concerned with membership, receiving the monetary blessings, and building the biggest churches possible. All these things are great, but not at the expense of the influence we lose from ill-gotten wealth, from manipulation, and from pulpit entertainment rather than real ministry. Many times we find members who can't see past a Sunday morning worship service and, if the truth was to be told, have not really been delivered from the chains of the enemy.

We have churches filled with great minds, talented orators with grand ideas, and orderly business, but no power! Power is our birthmark. When we receive God's Spirit, we are given power.

The church has always been associated with power. This power is not beyond our reach. In fact, it is just beyond our ego, our agenda, our tradition, our mindset, our program. It is so close.

A mediocre, watered-down, counterfeit version of the gospel is being preached. This erroneous doctrine dares not challenge the immorality that plagues the church and our society. Rather, it covenants with and affirms the culture.

We must understand that if we will ever be the church that God ordained, there must be in a shift in our thinking, our living, and our faith.

As a pastor, I have found myself frustrated about the lack of response to the word of God and the lack of intensity, commitment, and passion for ministry. But the fact remains that God is the judge, and He will separate the tares from the wheat, the real from the fake, and the authentic from the counterfeit.

Though some may take it lightly, the fact remains that God is calling His people to Himself. To His will. To His way. To His plan. To His faith. Our society and culture are sending the message that Jesus is an option rather than a necessity. Many of the views that we are embracing as a nation are in total contradiction to the Word of God. Sadly, many confessing Christians are being ensnared by an erroneous doctrine and conforming to the very world we are responsible to win.

God is calling for a people that will not compromise His truth nor cower down at the threats of a defeated enemy, regardless of how he manifests himself. I am one of the voices pleading with this generation. The alarm is being sounded, but the soldiers are in the enemy's camp. Who will hear, who will respond? Will you answer the call of faith?

OFF THE PAGES AND INTO YOUR LIFE: A TIME OF PERSONAL REFLECTION

Political correctness can lead spirit to spiritual incorrectness. We are called to draw the line. In doing so, we may not be popular in the sight of men, but we will be pleasing in the sight of God.

Do not become distracted by what's going on in the culture. Let your focus be on pleasing God. When Christ returns, He will separate the wheat from the tares, the sheep from the goats, and the righteous from the unrighteous. I challenge you speak the truth (in love) at all times.

The Prayer of Faith

Father, the world is embracing things that you do not. I pray when the temptation to compromise presents itself, you will remind me that I must be hot or cold, for you or against you. I take a bold stand to remain faithful and committed to the truth. I not only pray for myself, I pray for every Christian, every leader, every church and every person. Open up our hearts to receive you. Help us to represent you well, even in perilous times. Help us to be light in darkness. We truly need you. In Jesus name. Amen.

www.ingramcontent.com/pod-product-compliance
Lightning Source LLC
Chambersburg PA
CBHW070519090426
42735CB00012B/2841